TUSKEGEE AIRMEN

Matt Doeden

Lerner Publications ◆ Minneapolis

Content consultant: Daniel L. Haulman, PhD, Chief, Organizational
Histories Team, Air Force Historical Research Agency

Lerner Publications Company
A division of Lerner Publishing Group, Inc.
241 First Avenue North
Minneapolis, MN 55401 USA

For reading levels and more information, look up this title at
www.lernerbooks.com.

Main body text set in Aptifer Slab LT Pro Regular 11.5/18.
Typeface provided by Linotype AG.

Library of Congress Cataloging-in-Publication Data

Names: Doeden, Matt, author.
Title: Tuskegee Airmen / Matt Doeden.
Description: Minneapolis : Lerner Publications, 2018. | Series: Heroes of
    World War II | Includes bibliographical references and index.
Identifiers: LCCN 2017038558 (print) | LCCN 2017039594 (ebook) |
    ISBN 9781541521599 (eb pdf) | ISBN 9781541521490 (lb : alk. paper)
Subjects: LCSH: United States. Army Air Forces. Fighter Group,
    332nd—History—Juvenile literature. | United States. Army Air
    Forces. Bombardment Group, 477th—History—Juvenile literature. |
    World War, 1939–1945—Participation, African American—Juvenile
    literature. | World War, 1939–1945—Aerial operations, American—
    Juvenile literature. | African American air pilots—Juvenile literature. |
    Tuskegee Army Air Field (Ala.)—Juvenile literature.
Classification: LCC D810.N4 (print) | LCC D810.N4 D64 2018 (ebook) | DDC
    940.54/4973—dc23

LC record available at https://lccn.loc.gov/2017038558

Manufactured in the United States of America
1-44378-34643-11/29/2017

CONTENTS

INTRODUCTION
MISSION TO BERLIN

Lieutenant Roscoe Brown sat at the controls of his
P-51 Mustang fighter plane as it took off from Italy on
March 24, 1945. World War II (1939–1945) raged across
Europe. The Allied nations, including the United States,
Britain, and others, were closing in on Germany and

the Axis powers. Brown's unit of African American pilots was part of the Tuskegee Airmen, the first black combat pilots in US military history.

Brown knew that this would be one of his biggest **missions** of the war. US B-17 bombers were headed to Berlin, Germany—the heart of enemy territory—to destroy a German tank factory. Brown's unit had to protect the bombers at all costs.

A group of Fifteenth Air Force P-51s fly from Italy to complete a mission.

Four P-51 Mustangs fly in formation over Italy in 1945.

As the bombers neared Berlin, Brown saw several streaks in the sky. A group of German Me-262 fighters was coming in fast. The Me-262s were newer and much faster than the P-51s.

Brown acted quickly. He ordered his unit to drop their heavy extra fuel tanks and fight. The **dogfight** was on. Brown put himself between the attacking Me-262s and the US bombers. One of the German planes came straight for him.

"I pulled up at him . . . and fired three long bursts," Brown later wrote. It was a hit.

"Almost immediately, the pilot bailed out from about 24,500 feet (7,468 m). I saw flames burst from the [jets] of the enemy aircraft."

The Me-262 went down. All around Brown, his fellow pilots were fighting the German planes. Two more Tuskegee Airmen pilots brought down enemy planes. The German attack had failed, and the US mission continued. Only a few years earlier, many had doubted black pilots' ability to fly in combat. Those who saw Brown and his fellow Tuskegee Airmen in action no longer had any doubts.

Brown salutes a class at Air Command and Staff College, an air force school in Montgomery, Alabama, in 2015.

CHAPTER 1
THE TUSKEGEE EXPERIMENT

Racism was widespread in the United States when
World War II erupted in Europe in 1939. Many white
people saw black people as less than human. Laws in
many states segregated, or separated, black people and
white people. They couldn't use the same bathrooms,
attend the same schools, or eat in the same restaurants.

A class of white pilots walks past the
planes they are learning to fly in
San Diego in 1939.

The military was segregated too. No black pilots had ever flown for the US military. Many military leaders believed that black pilots lacked the intelligence needed to be combat pilots.

Wyoming senator Henry H. Schwartz disagreed. In 1939 Schwartz fought for a law that allowed for the training of black pilots. The law passed, yet the military did not make any changes. Schwartz visited General Henry H. Arnold, the chief of the Army Air Corps. Schwartz demanded that Arnold follow through with the new law. In January 1941, the War Department announced that it was going to form a new unit. All the pilots in the unit would be black.

Senator Henry H. Schwartz, 1939

9

TRAINING

The 99th Pursuit Squadron was officially formed in March 1941. The first training class in the program included just thirteen **cadets**. They studied subjects such as **navigation** and **meteorology**. They practiced flying in trainer planes such as the AT-6. The training was difficult. Only five of the original thirteen cadets completed it to earn their wings, or officially become pilots.

The first five African American pilots walk with their flight instructor, Lieutenant L. M. Long (*center*).

Benjamin O. Davis Jr.

Captain Benjamin O. Davis Jr. was one of them. He
had experienced racism while studying at the army's
West Point Academy a few years earlier. He understood
that people would be watching the black pilots extra
closely. Davis later became the leader of the 99th. He
told his pilots that he wouldn't allow any **hotdogging**.
He wanted them to focus on teamwork and on
completing their missions.

Colonel Noel Parrish

A NEW VOICE

By 1942 many cadets had become frustrated. They were treated poorly compared with white cadets. Then Colonel Noel Parrish took over. Parrish treated the cadets with respect. He tore down signs at the base that separated white and black pilots into different areas. He brought in black celebrities such as singer Ella Fitzgerald to improve **morale**.

Many say Parrish saved the Tuskegee program. The men thrived under his command. Even though he was white and never went to combat with his men, many see him as a key member of the Tuskegee Airmen.

Europe and Surrounding Areas during World War II

NORTH ATLANTIC OCEAN

UNITED KINGDOM

IRELAND

NORWAY

SWEDEN

FINLAND

DENMARK

NETHERLANDS

HOLLAND

ESTONIA

LATVIA

LITHUANIA

EAST PRUSSIA

Berlin

GERMANY

POLAND

SOVIET UNION

BELGIUM

CZECHOSLOVAKIA

FRANCE

AUSTRIA

HUNGARY

SWITZERLAND

ROMANIA

PORTUGAL

SPAIN

YUGOSLAVIA

Adriatic Sea

ITALY

BULGARIA

N

GREECE

SICILY

ALBANIA

TUNISIA

NORTH AFRICA

Miles
0 100 200 300

0 200 400
Kilometers

International border
Airmen mission locations
Europe
Non-Europe land

13

CHAPTER 2
ESCORT SPECIALISTS

Once the first waves of Tuskegee Airmen had graduated and earned their wings as US fighter pilots, the army had to decide what to do with them. Many in the army resisted the idea of **deploying** the black pilots. All pilots are officers, or high-ranking leaders in the military. So black pilots

The 99th Fighter Squadron was the first unit of Tuskegee Airmen. It was later one of four Tuskegee fighter squadrons.

Members of the 332nd Fighter Group wear flight gear while stationed in Italy in 1945.

would outrank many white soldiers. General Arnold described that as "an impossible social problem."

Yet the army needed every fighting man it could get. In April 1943, the all-black 99th Fighter Squadron went to North Africa. They were later assigned to the 332nd Fighter Group in Italy. They began flying missions over Italy and Germany. Soon they became known for one specialty: **escort** missions.

HISTORIC FIRST

Lieutenant Charles B. Hall sat at the controls to his P-40 Warhawk on July 2, 1943. Hall and the 99th Fighter Squadron soared through the skies over Sicily, an island off the coast of Italy. Their mission was to escort B-25 bombers on a bombing mission. The bombers were large, slow, and easy to attack.

Hall sits in the cockpit of his P-40 Warhawk.

An Fw-190 flies over Germany. The German plane was considered one of the best fighter planes of World War II.

Suddenly, Hall spotted two dark specks growing larger against the bright sun. Two German Fw-190 fighter planes swooped in at 400 miles (644 km) an hour. The German fighters headed straight for the bombers.

Tuskegee pilots fly in formation in 1943.

Hall moved to **intercept**. When one of the Fw-190s banked left, Hall had his opening. He opened fire with the P-40's .50-caliber guns. The shells shredded the enemy plane. It burst into a ball of flame.

"It was . . . the first time I had seen the enemy close enough to shoot him," Hall said. "I followed him down and saw him crash. He raised a big cloud of dust."

Hall's shooting of the plane marked a historic first. It was the first time an enemy plane had been shot down by a black US pilot. The Tuskegee Airmen had arrived.

STEM HIGHLIGHT

The North American P-51 Mustang was one of the most important planes of World War II. The single-seat plane could work as a fighter or a light bomber. The most common kind was the P-51D. It had a supercharged V12 engine. It could reach speeds of 437 miles (703 km) an hour and an altitude of 41,900 feet (12,771 m).

CHAPTER 3
ON THE ATTACK

During their missions, Tuskegee Airmen also bombed enemy airfields and **strafed** ground targets. These attacks were among the most dangerous missions the Tuskegee Airmen flew.

Charles McGee in 2011

PLANES AND TRAINS

On August 24, 1944, Charles McGee was on an escort mission over Czechoslovakia, a country that separated in 1993 into two countries: the Czech Republic and Slovakia. McGee spotted a German Fw-190. He moved in and fired. McGee's shot clipped the plane, but it didn't go down. The chase was on. The wounded Fw-190 ducked, dodged, and swerved near the ground. McGee kept it within his aim.

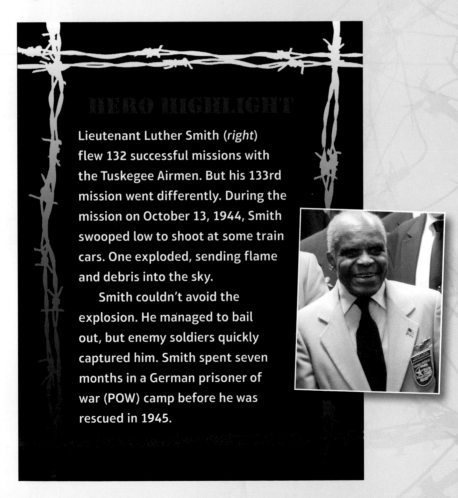

HERO HIGHLIGHT

Lieutenant Luther Smith (*right*) flew 132 successful missions with the Tuskegee Airmen. But his 133rd mission went differently. During the mission on October 13, 1944, Smith swooped low to shoot at some train cars. One exploded, sending flame and debris into the sky.

Smith couldn't avoid the explosion. He managed to bail out, but enemy soldiers quickly captured him. Smith spent seven months in a German prisoner of war (POW) camp before he was rescued in 1945.

The German pilot knew he was in trouble. He tried one last hard turn. But his plane couldn't handle it. The Fw-190 slammed into the ground.

McGee didn't stop there. Flying low, he spotted an enemy train. McGee opened fire, blasting the train cars before climbing back up to rejoin his unit.

DOGFIGHT

Airplanes filled the sky on October 12, 1944. Members of the 332nd Fighter Group were hitting ground targets in Hungary. Lieutenant Lee Archer and his squadron were cruising toward a target when German planes attacked.

Archer acted quickly as a huge dogfight erupted. He blasted a plane, pulled out of a sharp turn, and dove to follow a group of Me-109s. Once he had a clear view,

An Me-109 at the National Museum of the United States Air Force in Dayton, Ohio.

Archer opened fire. The wing of one of the Me-109s blew apart, sending the plane into a spin.

Archer targeted another Me-109. He blasted the plane's tail. Flames engulfed the Me-109. Its pilot immediately bailed out.

The dogfight lasted fifteen minutes. The pilots of the 332nd shot down nine planes, including Archer's three. It was one of the Tuskegee Airmen's most successful and memorable missions.

STEM HIGHLIGHT

Every World War II pilot feared crashing at sea. US pilots usually had gear to help them survive such crashes.

Some planes included emergency life rafts. The rafts could attach to a parachute pack. Once in the water, pilots used canisters of air to inflate the rafts. Rafts also carried sea markers. These markers left blotches of color on the surface of the water. Rescue planes could see them from far away.

CHAPTER 4
CASUALTIES OF WAR

Serving as a World War II fighter pilot was dangerous. The Tuskegee Airmen faced enemy fire as well as mechanical failure. Sixty-six pilots died during training and the war. Another thirty-two were captured and held prisoner.

Tuskegee Airmen attend a meeting in 1945.

SHOT DOWN

On August 12, 1944, Alexander Jefferson was part of a mission to strafe enemy ground targets. He watched as two of his squad mates dove low and hit their targets. Jefferson guided his plane toward his target, an air control tower.

Suddenly an antiaircraft shell blasted through the floor of Jefferson's plane. Jefferson tried to pull up and out of danger. But he had to bail out at the last moment. His squad mates believed that he was dead.

Alexander Jefferson, 2012

Stalag Luft III was a POW camp run by the German air force until April 1945. The camp held captured Allied pilots.

Jefferson was alive, but enemy troops captured him. He became a POW. Jefferson remained in a POW prison until April 1945. The conditions were harsh, but Jefferson survived and returned home.

GOING HOME

US soldiers, sailors, and airmen returned home as heroes. Yet the Tuskegee Airmen came home to a nation that was still deeply divided across racial lines. The bravery of African American servicemen, including the Tuskegee Airmen, was helping to change that, however. Three years after the war, President Harry Truman signed Executive Order 9981. The order said that everyone in the military would receive equal treatment and opportunity. People of different races would no longer be separated into race-based groups or squadrons. It was one step among many in the battle for equality among Americans of all races, and the Tuskegee Airmen played an important role in making it a reality.

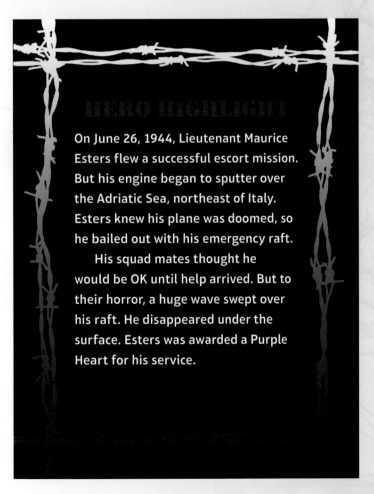

HERO HIGHLIGHT

On June 26, 1944, Lieutenant Maurice Esters flew a successful escort mission. But his engine began to sputter over the Adriatic Sea, northeast of Italy. Esters knew his plane was doomed, so he bailed out with his emergency raft.

His squad mates thought he would be OK until help arrived. But to their horror, a huge wave swept over his raft. He disappeared under the surface. Esters was awarded a Purple Heart for his service.

TIMELINE

September 1, 1939   World War II begins.

March 22, 1941   The 99th Pursuit Squadron, which would be the first black flying unit in history, was activated.

December 7, 1941   Japanese pilots bomb Pearl Harbor, Hawaii. The United States enters World War II.

April 2, 1943   The 99th Fighter Squadron ships out to North Africa to become the US Army's first black combat pilots.

July 2, 1943   Charles B. Hall shoots down a German Fw-190, becoming the first black US pilot to kill an enemy in battle.

June 26, 1944   Lieutenant Maurice Esters is lost at sea after his plane crashes in the Adriatic Sea following a successful escort mission.

August 23, 1944   Charles McGee downs a German Fw-190 in the skies over Czechoslovakia.

October 12, 1944   The pilots of the 332nd Fighter Group down nine planes in a dogfight over the skies of Germany.

March 24, 1945	Roscoe Brown shoots down a German Me-262 during an escort mission over Berlin, Germany.
May 7, 1945	Germany formally surrenders, ending the European part of World War II.
August 14, 1945	Shortly after the atomic bombings of Hiroshima and Nagasaki, Japan announces that it will surrender. World War II ends.

Source Notes

6 Robert F. Dorr, "Tuskegee Airmen vs. Mc 262s," *Defense Media Network*, February 25, 2013, http://www.defensemedianetwork .com/stories/tuskegee-airmen-vs-me-262s/.

6 Ibid.

15 Lynn M. Homan and Thomas Reilly, *Black Knights: The Story of the Tuskegee Airmen* (Gretna, LA: Pelican, 2001), 71.

18 Charles E. Francis, *The Tuskegee Airmen: The Men Who Changed a Nation* (Wellesley, MA: Branden Books, 2002), 67.

Glossary

cadets: military students

deploying: putting soldiers into combat situations

dogfight: an aerial battle between two or more fighter planes

escort: to travel with and protect someone or something

hotdogging: the act of performing aerial stunts to show off

intercept: to move between an attacker and its target

meteorology: the study of weather

missions: military tasks

morale: the feelings and goodwill of troops

navigation: determining one's location and following a route

strafed: attacked a ground target from a low-flying airplane

FURTHER INFORMATION

BBC: World War II
http://www.bbc.co.uk/schools/primaryhistory/world_war2/

Ducksters: African Americans in World War II
http://www.ducksters.com/history/world_war_ii/african
_americans_in_ww2.php

Lusted, Marcia Amidon. *Eyewitness to the Tuskegee Airmen.*
Mankato, MN: Child's World, 2016.

National Geographic Kids: Ten Facts about World War II
http://www.ngkids.co.uk/history/world-war-two

Otfinoski, Steven. *World War II.* New York: Scholastic, 2017.

Owens, Lisa L. *Women Pilots of World War II.* Minneapolis: Lerner
Publications, 2019.

Shea, John M. *The Tuskegee Airmen.* New York: Gareth Stevens,
2015.

Tuskegee Airmen
http://tuskegeeairmen.org/

The Tuskegee Airmen National Historical Museum
http://www.tuskegeemuseum.org

INDEX

PHOTO ACKNOWLEDGMENTS

The images in this book are used with the permission of: iStockphoto.com/akinshin (barbed wire backgrounds throughout); iStockphoto.com/ElementalImaging, p. 1 (camouflage background); National Archives, pp. 4–5, 18; Library of Congress (LC-DIG-ppmsca-13268), p. 6; US Air Force Photograph by Donna L. Burnett, p. 7; Keystone-France/Getty Images, p. 8; Library of Congress (LC-DIG-hec-26038), p. 9; Library of Congress (LC-USZ62-94039), pp. 10, 28; US Air Force photo, p. 11; US Air Force photo (CC 1.0 PDM), p. 12; © Laura Westlund/Independent Picture Service, p. 13; US Air Force photo/National Museum of the United States Air Force, pp. 14, 16, 22; Library of Congress (LC-DIG-ppmsca-13248, p. 15; Willi Ruge/ullstein bild/Getty Images, p. 17; US Air Force/Wikimedia Commons, pp. 19, 29 (left); US Air Force photo by Staff Sgt. Vernon Young Jr., p. 20; Chris Maddaloni/Roll Call/Getty Images, p. 21; iStock.com/aaron007, pp. 21, 27 (wire frame); San Diego Air & Space Museum Archives/flickr.com, p. 23; Library of Congress (LC-DIG-ppmsca-13260), pp. 24, 29 (right); © US Embassy London/flickr.com (CC BY-ND 2.0), p. 25; Hulton Archive/Getty Images, p. 26.

Cover: US Air Force (Tuskegee Airmen); iStockphoto.com/akinshin (barbed wire background); iStockphoto.com/ElementalImaging (camouflage background); iStockphoto.com/MillefloreImages (flag background).